30 WAYS
A HUSBAND CAN
BLESS HIS WIFE

JOHN TRENT, PH.D.

AspirePress

Torrance, California

AspirePress

30 Ways a Husband Can Bless His Wife
Copyright © 2015 John Trent
All rights reserved.
Aspire Press, an imprint of Rose Publishing, Inc.
4733 Torrance Blvd., #259
Torrance, California 90503 USA
www.aspirepress.com
Register your book at www.aspirepress.com/register

*Special thanks to Kari Trent and Tamara Love
for their assistance in making these books possible.*

The views and opinions expressed in this book are those of the author(s) and do not necessarily express the views of Aspire Press, nor is this book intended to be a substitute for mental health treatment or professional counseling.

All scripture quotations, unless otherwise indicated, are taken from the New American Standard Bible®, Copyright © 1960, 1962, 1963, 1968, 1971, 1972, 1973, 1975, 1977, 1995 by The Lockman Foundation Used by permission.

Scripture quotations marked (NIV) taken from the Holy Bible, New International Version®, NIV®. Copyright ©1973, 1978, 1984, 2011 by Biblica, Inc.™ Used by permission of Zondervan. All rights reserved worldwide. www. zondervan.com The "NIV" and "New International Version" are trademarks registered in the United States Patent and Trademark Office by Biblica, Inc.™

Scripture quotations marked (ESV) taken from The Holy Bible, English Standard Version Copyright © 2001 by Crossway Bibles, a publishing ministry of Good News Publishers.

Printed in the United States of America
010715RRD

CONTENTS

THE VALUE OF LITTLE CHOICES

THERE ARE LOTS of choices we make each day that really aren't that significant. Turkey sandwich or ham. Soup or salad. Try to get around traffic or sit it out in the lane we're in and tough it out. Watch the late summary on ESPN or head to bed and get some extra sleep. Those choices have minimal impact on our life today or our future tomorrow.

But there are choices that can make a real difference in our life today and tomorrow. Like the choice to be a man who looks to God's Word to be the moral compass of his life, instead of just emotionally flipping a coin or going with our gut feeling or polling our friends to find out what they think. Like choosing to follow Jesus each day. Like choosing, with God's help and Spirit, to be a better man today than we were yesterday. Like choosing to perform small actions that can be an incredibly powerful tool for adding love and life to your marriage as a whole and to your wife's life and future in particular.

Those are the kinds of choices we make each day that really *can* make a *real* difference in who we are today and the man we'll be tomorrow. As the great scholar and Christian C. S. Lewis wrote in his book *Mere Christianity*, "Remember, we Christians think man lives forever. Therefore, what really matters are those little markers or twists on the central, inside part of the soul, which are going to turn it, in the long run, into a healthy or hellish creature."

> **SMALL ACTIONS CAN BE A POWERFUL TOOL FOR ADDING LOVE AND LIFE TO YOUR MARRIAGE.**

It is indeed those little things we choose to do in our spiritual and personal life—*including the way we treat our wife at home when no one but our God and our children are watching*—that will set our course for future actions and a healthy relationship. Those small choices—which is what this book is all about—are bound up in what C. S. Lewis called "one of the great secrets":

> *When you are behaving as if you loved someone, you will presently come to love him. . . . Good and evil both increase at compound interest. That is why the little decisions you and I make every day are of such infinite importance. The smallest good act today is the capture of a strategic point from which, a few months later, you may be able to go on to victories you never dreamed of. An apparently trivial indulgence in lust or anger today is the loss of a ridge or railway line or bridgehead from which the enemy may launch an attack otherwise impossible.*

The incredible power of little choices is absolutely true for both our faith and our life. And guess where our faith gets lived out first and last.

It's in our home where we live out our faith, and where those small choices add up to shape our soul—and our marriage. That just makes sense.

Most of us don't start our day at church (unless we live in a parsonage). We may regularly go to church. But it is in our home, where we have the most important earthly relationships, that the rubber meets the road. That's where you and I will make choices and live out the corresponding actions of those choices. Where we will either move closer to our spouse or further away. Where we will choose to have a good attitude or a poor one. Where we will choose to move towards God's best or away from it.

THE BLESSING IS SOMETHING THAT CAN BE GIVEN AND EXPERIENCED IN SMALL WAYS EVERY DAY.

WHAT THE BLESSING IS

THE BLESSING IS about unconditional love and acceptance of a person. It is about

- ○ seeing the potential in someone,
- ○ assigning great value to that person,
- ○ reaching out with meaningful touch,
- ○ speaking words of blessing over them, and
- ○ demonstrating an active commitment to that person.

The blessing is for *all* relationships. Here we'll focus on specific ways that a husband can bless his wife. The relationship between husband and wife is one that is revered in Scripture. Husbands and wives are both instructed to put effort into their relationship. Marriage is to be protected and honored by those who believe in Jesus Christ, and it provides a picture of the sacrificial relationship between Jesus and his bride, the church.

The influence of a husband upon his wife is phenomenal. Will you be the kind of husband who builds up his wife and encourages her to be all that God created her to be?

I am so grateful to have an excellent wife. Cindy is my best friend, and she has stuck with me through thick, thin, and thinner. While neither of us grew up in a Christian home, we both were committed to establishing our marriage with Christ at the center and raising our family around the truth that Jesus is more precious than anything. Cindy has been a voice of wisdom for me through many career and personal decisions, and I would not be where I am today without her continual encouragement and support. Cindy believes in the blessing, and we have actively given each other the blessing throughout the years of our relationship.

Having someone in our lives who believes in us and walks with us through life's challenges while cheering us on to be all that God created us to be can inspire us to pursue more than we might think is possible. I hope that your wife is that person for you and that you are that person for your wife.

A Culture of Blessing

Of course, the act of a husband's giving of the blessing isn't just reserved for a once-in-a-lifetime momentous occasion. You can bless your wife in small ways every day! In fact, it's all these small, specific, positive ways you'll learn about that can help you as a husband create what we call a culture of blessing in your home!

Think about a culture like setting a thermostat in your home. Try living in Chicago in February and setting the thermostat at 20 degrees throughout the house. No matter where you go in that home, the atmosphere, or culture, communicates one thing: it's cold! Your whole focus isn't on relating to others or being free to do things inside; your focus is on getting warm! But now set the thermostat at 72 degrees and watch life warm up and the focus of your family go from what's missing (heat) to all the things you *can do* as a family! You've added life (movement) to the home, because you've changed the thermostat (or culture)! And when you create a culture of blessing in the home, the entire family benefits. You all have the freedom to move towards God's best!

The Five Essential Elements

Let's get more specific about just what makes up the blessing. You'll see these elements pop up in the suggestions and examples that follow.

Throughout Scripture, five distinct elements usually characterized the blessing. First, the blessing began with a *meaningful touch*. The blessing continued with a *spoken message*, meaning the blessing was said or written out, so it was unmistakable. The third element of the blessing was how the words always expressed *high value*. Fourth, the giver of the blessing pictured a *special future* for the one being blessed. And then these four attitudes and actions were lived out and demonstrated through an *active commitment* to see the blessing come to pass in that person's life.

Each of these five elements contributes its own impact on your blessing.

Meaningful Touch (Lovingly Touch)

A *meaningful touch* was an important part of giving the blessing in the Old Testament. When Isaac blessed his son, he called him, saying, "Come near and kiss me, my son" (Genesis 27:26, ESV). Isaac's words "come near" actually translate as "come and embrace in a bear hug." Jesus blessed the little children who came to him, "[taking] them in his arms and . . . laying his hands on them" (Mark 10:16, ESV). The benefits of touch are enormous—physically, emotionally, and spiritually. In marriage, meaningful touch is a primary means of communicating intimacy.

Research has shown, time and again, the incredible benefits of touch. For example, premature babies who are touched and held gain weight dramatically faster than those who aren't. (Touch isn't the reason why you or your wife has gained weight. Those studies on weight gain and touch only work with babies!) When someone puts their hands on another's shoulders—like you giving your wife a back rub—her blood pressure will go down (even if yours doesn't!). Touch has many physical benefits, but perhaps most important, without a word being spoken, your touch is an incredibly powerful way to say, "I love you. I care for you."

Spoken Message (Say It!)

A *spoken message* has the power to build up or tear down a person's sense of worth. Our words hold great power, and the blessing acknowledges this through the spoken message. In the Bible, a blessing was invalid unless it was spoken. In the book of James, we see multiple pictures of the power of the tongue. The tongue is described as a bit that gives direction to a horse, a rudder that turns a ship, and a spreading fire (James 3:1–6). Each of these pictures shows us the potential of the tongue to build up or tear down. Will your tongue be one that encourages or belittles your wife? The apostle Paul challenged the church of Ephesus with these words: "Let no corrupting talk come out of your mouths, but only such as is good for building up, as fits the occasion, that it may give grace to those who hear" (Ephesians 4:29, ESV). Let your spoken words to your wife be words of blessing so that she may experience grace.

I remember one of my mentors, Dr. Howards Hendricks, once telling me about a counseling session he had that he never forgot. He had been trying to encourage a husband to be more verbally affirming with his wife. When the doctor challenged the husband about the fact that he had never once said "I love you" to his wife since they got married over thirty years before, the man thundered at him from across the room, "I told my wife I loved

> **LET YOUR SPOKEN WORDS TO YOUR WIFE BE WORDS OF BLESSING SO THAT SHE MAY EXPERIENCE GRACE.**

her on the day we were married and it stands until I revoke it!"

That statement is wrong on so many levels! Just listen to the pride and anger dripping from those words. And the fact that at any time, his one-time statement could be withdrawn? Revoked? That man might have felt that his love still echoed after thirty plus years, but he was dead wrong. When you really love someone—even if you grew up not often hearing that love as a child or seeing your parents use loving words to encourage each other—you need to say it!

In the Scriptures, the word *love* occurs well over three hundred times, and in fact, the Bible says that "God is love" (1 John 4:8, 16). In the Gospel of John, we're told that "the Word [love] became flesh and dwelt among us, and we have seen his glory, glory as of the only Son from the Father, full of grace and truth" (John 1:14, ESV). God didn't express his love just once. He sent his Son to embody his word, so we couldn't miss it! Just think about the fact that the only time the heavenly Father speaks to his Son on earth (at the baptism of Jesus and again at the Transfiguration), he says, "This is my beloved Son" (Matthew 3:17; 17:5). *Beloved!*

> PEOPLE WHO FEEL LOVED ARE HAPPIER AND THEY MAKE BETTER DECISIONS.

If anyone says to you, "Well, don't praise your wife or kids too much, because they'll get a swelled head," tell them this: The world is going to tell your wife and your kids in a hundred different ways that they're worthless and have no value. People who feel loved are happier and they make better decisions. It's best to praise your wife (or child) for persistence and their ability to stick with a difficult task, rather than intellect. Complementing their effort in the face of challenges is always a good. In fact, scientists have shown that applauding time, perseverance and courage is better than praising intellect, attractiveness, or talent.

Husband, praising your wife works wonders—so say it!

In the book Song of Solomon, King Solomon's bride began their relationship feeling incredibly insecure and unworthy, particularly because while Solomon had none other than King David as his father and had been raised in a palace, her father apparently was gone and her brothers had forced her to work in the fields (Song of Solomon 1:5–6).

She feels so down about herself that as the book begins, she says to her husband-to-be, "Do not gaze at me" (Song of Solomon 1:6, ESV). She feels so unworthy, so worthless, she can't even fathom what he would see in her.

Yet listen to how that same woman describes herself later in the book: "I am a rose of Sharon, a lily of the valleys" (Song of Solomon 2:1, ESV). That is one of the greatest pictures in all romantic literature of how this wise man changed her heart. And he did so by pouring on her spoken words of praise—by believing she had incredible value (no matter what her brothers felt) and being willing to say it!

Husband, forty times in eight short chapters in the Song of Solomon, he praises her. In fairness, twenty-four times in eight chapters she praises him. We need encouragement and affirmation from our wives as well. But think about your job of laying down your life for your wife. Of serving her. Blessing her. To have a wife go from saying "Don't even look at me" to "Put me on display" is something you can do as well with your wife!

Attach High Value (Express High Value)

What kind of words are you to speak or write down for your spouse so that you might bless her? Those that *express high value*. To value something is to attach great importance to it. In blessing your spouse, you are choosing to ascribe great worth to her, acknowledging that she is valuable to the Lord and to you. This is important, even in times of conflict or struggle. Husband, your relationship with your wife will face times of great difficulty! But in the times when you may not feel the value of your spouse, choosing to speak words of high value to her will realign your own perspective and encourage her to see her value as well.

I'll be giving you several suggestions for blessing your wife that will help bring a deep sense of acceptance and appreciation as you express high value about who your wife is and how God has directed her life.

Picture a Special Future (See Potential)

With our *meaningful touch*, with our choice to use a *spoken message*, and by attaching words with *high value* to our spouse, we lay the foundation to help us picture a *special future* for them as well. As we attach value to a person, we can see their potential and envision the great ways in which they might impact the world for Christ. By paying attention to the strengths your wife exhibits, you can see how God might use her unique gifts to serve others and how her strengths might benefit her relationships and future endeavors. Encourage your spouse through picturing a special future for her in which God uses her gifts to impact others.

It's amazing how often and how well other people can see something we're good at—or have potential in—when we just don't see it. Let me give you an example. There was a girl I went to grade school with. She had a beautiful older sister—a "stop traffic" older sister—who won every award at school. But Lynda, the girl I knew, was totally ignored. But then right at the end of high school, one person heard Lynda sing. And that person encouraged her by telling her that she had a really great voice. And that person talked her into taking singing lessons. And that led to her trying out for a talent show . . . and then trying out for a pageant . . . and that pageant led to the Miss Arizona pageant (which she won) . . . then to the Miss World pageant (where she reached the semi-finals) ... and then to television (where she eventually starred in her own program). You probably even know my grade-school friend, Lynda Carter, but you probably know her as Wonder Woman.

I knew Lynda pretty well in high school, but I marveled at the person she became when someone (not me) pointed out to her the potential she had to bless others with her singing.

Your wife needs you to tell her and give her a picture of the potential you see in her that can lead to a special future. OK, not necessarily winning a beauty pageant or starring in a television show. But her believing in her potential because she's heard it from you—that she could do more than she ever dreamed—if she just believed what you told her she could do. That God in her could do more than she could ever do by herself.

Later on you'll learn some practical ways to spot potential you can praise and help to develop in your wife (like a coach looking at a player and seeing who they can become). And you'll learn some ways you can demonstrate to your wife that you're here for the future, for the long haul. As far as you're concerned, the two of you will be together in the future no matter what and "as long as you both shall live." Seeing the potential in your wife is an amazingly powerful way of adding security and strength, vision and hope, energy and life to your wife. So get busy looking for and communicating ways you can encourage your wife's potential—that special future that she'll be sharing with you as the two of you hang together, forever!

Active Commitment (Be Committed)

The last element of the blessing really seals the deal, as the one giving the blessing demonstrates an *active commitment* to see the blessing come to pass in that person's life. Words have to be accompanied by action. The blessing is not merely spoken but lived— even when it's hard.

Husband, you bless your spouse when you sacrifice yourself, your pride, your demands, your wants, for her. It's in dying to self that you'll find the opposite—life! Just like Jesus modeled for us! That's a key part of this whole idea of active commitment, the call to be committed. Be committed in sacrificial ways. In big and small ways you can say by your actions, not just your words, that your wife has your blessing and that you love her and the God who gave her to you.

As you are intentional about connecting with

and blessing your wife today, you will be adding layer after layer of love and acceptance into her life that she'll be able to draw strength from when she faces challenges each and every day. The marriage relationship is under constant stress, but when you consistently strive to give your wife the blessing, you will work to create a culture of blessing within your marriage.

I live in Arizona, which is largely made up of desert. You may feel that your marriage is a desert—dry, hot, and maybe even exhausting! As you seek to give your wife the blessing and make your home and environment a culture of blessing, your marriage can become a tropical oasis rather than a desert. I am constantly challenging people to

> **YOU CAN SAY BY YOUR ACTIONS, NOT JUST YOUR WORDS, THAT YOUR WIFE HAS YOUR BLESSING.**

make small two-degree changes in their lives and watch as those changes impact the overall experience. You don't steer a huge cruise liner by jerking the steering wheel; gently turn the wheel in small increments and the direction (and destination!) of the boat is completely altered. In that same way, know that every small effort you make to bless your wife adds up to lasting impact in her heart.

Here's a way to remember all the various elements that make up the blessing—a way I teach to people, through an acronym: BLESS. While the elements are rearranged from the order in our discussion, this is an easy way to remember all five elements:

B stands for "be committed" (active commitment)

L stands for "lovingly touch" (meaningful touch)

E stands for "express value" (high value)

S stands for "see potential" (special future)

S stands for "say it!" (spoken message)

Show-and-Tell

Any teacher knows that show-and-tell can be even more powerful than just tell. So in the pages that follow, I want to show you thirty simple, practical ways that husbands have used to pass on the blessing to their wife.

You certainly aren't limited to these thirty, but I hope they will act as a springboard for your efforts to pass on the blessing to your wife. You will see that each suggestion incorporates a variety of the five elements of the blessing. Some focus on using spoken words. Others incorporate a meaningful touch or help you to picture a special future. In some of the examples and occasions discussed, you'll see where all five come together in one activity or suggestion! And, yes, some aspects of each blessing might be easier for you to give than others. But the cumulative result of implementing all five elements of the blessing will help your wife in so many ways—emotionally, physically, spiritually.

You goal isn't to try and mark a checklist as you use each example. And there's no need to do each one perfectly. Nor does passing on a blessing have to result in the best evening ever or some huge emotional response from your wife. What you're looking to do is choose to layer in the blessing—to create that 72-degree culture of caring, acceptance, commitment, and courage in your home. It's not about perfection or emotion or doing something just right. It is about jumping in and going all in on being a husband who is going to choose to bless his wife.

Over time, by choosing to bless your wife, you'll start creating that culture of blessing in your home. You'll see the blessing become a habit that enriches your home and eats discouragement and bad attitudes.

Your wife deserves to know that you're crazy about her! Beyond that, your wife deserves to know that *Jesus* is crazy about her as well. It can change her life today and point her towards a special future tomorrow.

WHAT THE BLESSING DOES[1]

LET ME SHARE four reasons why the blessing can make a transformational change in your home.

The blessing defies a toxic culture.

The blessing runs full force against the tide of a busy society. With parents working long hours to make ends meet—or simply preoccupied with their own agendas—many children grow up today struggling with what experts call *attachment disorder*. That's the failure to create significant bonds in relationships. As adults, they stumble down the road in relationships with a deep desire for connection, but with the ever-present feeling that they just don't know how to build loving, lasting relationships. They step back from what they want most because they've never seen what it looks like to have someone step toward them.

Blessing your wife is about intentionally taking those steps—big and small—toward her. The blessing offers a way of reclaiming connection with your spouse, no matter how many hours the demands of our busy world try to siphon out of your day.

The blessing can help open a closed heart.

Christianity is about a relationship. When we trust in God, we enter into a relationship with our Creator. The blessing is all about building relationships! When you give your wife the blessing, you are helping her take hold of relational tools that can not only help her connect with you and other people, but can also open her heart to a new or strengthened relationship with Jesus.

The blessing can help free your spouse from a wounded past.

We all have good and bad in our past. Even adults who grew up in the best and most loving of homes might still carry with them a certain amount of hurt or disappointment.

Children don't have the maturity or understanding to deal with hurt and pain, so they develop self-protective mechanisms. They latch on to anything that they think can protect them and help them cope: athletic prowess, academic success, good looks, video games and social media, even drugs or alcohol. Whatever works, they want to repeat. By the time they grow up, they may have created layer upon layer of self-protection. But these layers have a

A WIFE WHO RECEIVES THE BLESSING CAN BE FREED TO PURSUE GOD'S BEST IN EVERY AREA OF HER LIFE.

shelf life! Success is fleeting. Looks fade. Addictive substances and activities don't satisfy deep longings.

None of these self-protective mechanisms offer real, unshakable, lasting confidence and connection.

The blessing offers an alternative to damaging coping methods and the life-suffocating layers of self-protection. Instead of keeping herself wrapped in self-protection, a wife who receives the blessing can be freed to pursue God's best in every area of her life. What would it look like if your spouse didn't have to live in fear of not out-doing others at work? If she didn't have to worry about acquiring all the status symbols someone else has? If she could move beyond issues that have held her back for years and finally make peace with her past? That can be another life-changing part of experiencing the blessing from God, from others, and from you.

The blessing is part of your calling.

Christians hear it from all corners today—from books, radio shows, websites, podcasts, and the pulpit. It's the call to a "sold-out" life of faith. It's the mission Jesus proclaimed for us: "Go therefore and make disciples" … everywhere! (Matthew 28:19, ESV).

But adopting this "missional" lifestyle that Christ called us to doesn't mean leaving your loved ones in the dust. Your family—your wife—is part of your calling. If you're not living out your faith and love for Christ with your family first, you have missed a huge first step!

If you find yourself too busy to give your wife the blessing because you're preoccupied with a "higher calling," you're missing the whole point of the gospel. The apostle Paul—a "missional" believer if there ever was one!—made it clear that "if anyone does not provide for his own, and especially for those of his household, he has denied the faith and is worse than an unbeliever" (1 Timothy 5:8). Building strong relational ties is part of your calling. The blessing can be one of your most important tools in ministering to your wife. And you just might find that your blessing will give her the confidence and encouragement to live a "sold-out" life for Christ along with you.

Now that you have a grasp on what the blessing really is and why giving it to your wife is so important, let's jump into thirty ways to give the blessing to your wife.

30 WAYS TO BLESS YOUR WIFE

1

Share-the-Wealth Blessing

 Be committed to spending as much on her and your children's needs as on your own wants and needs.

I'll never forget counseling one couple where the wife had filed for divorce because the husband had just bought his *third* set of high-end golf clubs. He wasn't a professional golfer, just a weekend hacker who wanted to impress his friends with the "latest and greatest" clubs. But that wasn't all the story. Linked with his spending thousands and thousands on his hobbies was his steadfast *no* when it came to spending money on his children or wife. Before she filed, he had told his wife it was "unnecessary" and a waste of money for their children to have money to play a sport at school—after all, they weren't going to be pros. (He, however, "needed" his new clubs because he "did business" on the course with his friends and business contacts.) When it came to spending money to get several needed repairs done around the house, he had told her, "No. *Period*." And the final blow for her came when he told her that there was no money for her to fly to see her sister who had just had a heart attack at age forty-five, but he could spend over $2,500 on his *third* set of golf clubs.

Husband, here are several ways you can choose to bless your wife by choosing to spend as much on her and the children as you do on yourself:

➲ Make sure you're spending more money on her and the kids than on your golf clubs (or on whatever hobby you pursue).

➲ Spend money on getting her a great winter coat, instead of just something she can get by on.

➲ Spend as much or more on her car tires as your own. That's your wife and children in that car. Your wheels are important, but her safety should come first.

➲ Ask your wife, "So what is it we need (not just want) to be saving for that's coming up that will help you or the kids?" Even if your wife isn't bringing in a paycheck, you add to her life when you make decisions based on what's best for her first. Even if you have to hit the ball off the first tee with an old driver.

➲ With your wife, agree to a dollar limit on what either of you can spend without having to call the other person and talk the purchase over with them. For my wife, Cindy, and me, the limit was $25 when we first got married. Even today it's $75. When you've talked through together where the money goes, you avoid having terrible arguments when the credit-card bill comes in each month. And you've chosen to bless her by making her needs and your children's needs more important than your own.

2

Symbols-of-Marriage Blessing

 As a marriage and family counselor, I will sometimes ask the kids if there is anything they'd like for Mom and Dad to think about or perhaps do differently. Sure, some kids say, "They need to let me stay up later" or "They need to let me watch more television." But I'll never forget one young girl saying to me, "I wish Daddy would quit throwing Mom away."

I didn't understand what she was saying and asked if she could explain. So she said, "When Daddy gets mad, he takes off his wedding ring and throws it away." The father explained that he didn't literally throw the ring away. But when he was angry, he'd take off his wedding ring and chuck it across the room so that it bounced off the wall or went down the hall. Later he'd pick it up, and eventually he'd put it back on. But what his child saw in his acting so childishly was his "throwing away" of his wife—and their future.

Husband, you bless your wife by being committed to honor the symbols of your marriage. And one way you can bless your wife is to treat the symbols of your marriage with honor. You may not realize it, but to most wives, the symbols of marriage are far more than just "things." The icons of your marriage, like your wedding ring, are living word pictures of how you value your marriage relationship. With this in mind, here are some ways to honor the symbols of your marriage:

➲ The next time you're shopping at the mall, go into a jewelry store, and while you're shopping, leave the wedding rings you each wear (get a receipt from the store, of course), and have the people at the jewelry store clean the rings (many jewelers will do this for free). It's amazing how my beat-up wedding ring will almost sparkle when I get it back, and I always proceed to wear it as proudly as the day I received it at the altar. And Cindy's ring, having been checked over to make sure the prongs on the diamond (my grandmother's diamond) are fine, shines like the day we were married as well. It's a small thing but a great way to say, "This symbol of our marriage means something to me."

➡ Take time on or near your anniversary (or anytime, actually) to go through your wedding album. I admit, for me this is painful. I had almost no money when we got married. I remember walking into the tuxedo store and after looking at the prices, I finally said, "Don't you have anything in the back that you're getting rid of or that you just can't rent that's cheaper?" He did. Now, every time I look at our wedding pictures, I see that incredibly ugly gray tux with the huge white stripe down the bell-bottom pants and the extra fluffy cuffs sticking out of the coat sleeves. *What was I thinking back then?!* But no matter what the pictures look like, talk about your joy that's captured in the pictures of that day. The people there. The way she looked so beautiful. The way she still does.

○ At your ten-year anniversary (or twenty or thirty or whatever year you choose), make a big deal out of renewing your vows in front of the kids and pets and friends and family. Tell your wife that you'd marry her all over again.

3

Be-the-Nurse Blessing

When our kids or I got sick, it was in my wife's nature to kick in and be the nurse. But when Cindy was sick, it was like the whole house fell apart! We'd bug her so much to get out of bed that it was like her feeling poorly didn't count! But when Cindy badly burned both her hands years ago, I learned that being the nurse for her could be a powerful way to build the blessing into our marriage.

Until Cindy's hands healed, I had to wash her hair, help her button her clothes, do the dishes, cook the food, help put medicine on her blistered hands—I had to be the nurse. And it didn't make me any less manly. Instead, it made me way more loving than I thought I could ever be. So here's some ways you can be the nurse when needed:

➲ Look for ways and times to help your wife when she or the kids are sick. You can do this by giving her a break if she needs it. Take over, so she can get a shower or grab dinner or go shopping while you watch a sick kid.

➲ Always be willing to go to the store and get the medicine, if she needs you to.

➲ When you can, really try hard to take time off from work and go to those doctor's appointments that your wife is worried about. Even if you have to take a vacation day or go a day without pay, if she's scared for herself or a child going to a particular doctor's appointment, be there with her.

➲ Make sure that your wife gets her physical. That you take time off so that she can go to the dentist. That you're willing to pay the money needed to get her whatever help she needs to cure whatever illness she might have. Yes, health care is expensive. But your wife, who you're looking to bless, is priceless.

4

Full-Time-Husband Blessing

 Here's what I tell literally every man who comes into my office for counseling: "From this day forward, you have *two* full time jobs."

If the man is already working two jobs, I tell him he now has *three* full-time jobs. You might think this discourages men. In fact, it pulls up something inside a man when you call him out. When you ask him to do more, not less (like that coach who kept blowing that whistle, having you do more wind sprints then you ever thought you could).

It's time for me to tell you to forget walking in the door to just rest so that you can go back to work. You *are* at work when you come home. You need to step up when you come home, instead of just putting your feet up and zoning out.

I'm not saying you aren't tired when you get home, but so is you wife. There is a time for rest, but that time is not the first hour after you hit the house after work. What I do is pull the car into the driveway and before I hit the garage-door button, I just sit there with my palms down on the top of my legs and I pray through my day. I figuratively dump out or shake off all the tough things about the day. The call that didn't come. The check that didn't show up. The huge project that's due, but I'm late on. It's out with the bad first. But then I turn my palms up and pray, "Lord, so now that I've dumped all that out, now fill my open palms with your love, patience, kindness, gentleness, and self-control. And Lord give me energy too, even if it's just for the next hour."

And then I get to work. And it never fails that during that first hour on deck, I find many ways to help and serve my wife—to bless her.

I know it might feel natural to kick up your feet and zone out for a while in front of the tube or disappear into the garage and spend all night on a hobby or finishing a task. After all, you've worked hard. And it might feel natural to let her do her thing (with the kids or her friends or TV). But that's stepping away. Remember, life is all about stepping towards her—about adding to her life—about being committed.

Long story short, at least until the kids are grown and gone, you're working double shifts as a godly man. Period. I guarantee you that the Lord will honor you for leaning in, not away from, your wife and children when you get home from work. And your wife will be blessed when you make that sacrifice to be there and not check out.

So bless your own life by stepping up and realizing that the first hour when you get home might often be like "the valley of the shadow of death"— when kids are hungry and grumpy and your wife is worn out from work and life—but ask God to fill you up for just one hour. Then you'll rest. And you'll be amazed at what happens because you didn't zone out.

5

Make-Meetings-Matter Blessing

 Show up at meetings that are important to your wife. This is an especially powerful way you can bless your wife. Your presence demonstrates that you are in this together, and that her priorities are important to you.

➲ Go with your wife to parent meetings at your child's school. My wife, Cindy, is an ESL first- and second-grade teacher. This past fall, she had twenty-two kids in her class. While it was bad enough that only three parents showed up for Parents Night, what was worse was that there wasn't one father among those three parents who did choose to come. That's pathetic. In short, as long as you aren't overseas and you won't lose your job if you take time off, choose to go to the Parents Night for each of your children. It will honor your children when you choose to have the commitment to go, but it is also a powerful way for you to say "I'm committed" to your wife and, with your wife, to your child's future.

➲ Go with your wife to your wife's favorite charity ball, auction, or celebration evening. There are two things Cindy is really passionate about: kids coming to Jesus, and helping pets that don't have a choice or voice. So guess what I've learned is a great way to be committed. If she asks me to go to the Young Life Banquet or the local Shelter Barbecue and Silent Auction, I make that part of my "second" job. Don't just send your wife to these sort of events, even if it's with a check. Go there with her. It's a great way to say that what she values matters to you and that she matters to you as well.

➲ Be willing to go with your wife to events put on by her side of the family. I know. That's even tougher for many of guys than going to a Parents Night. But it doesn't matter if you have nothing in common with your in-laws or her siblings. If your wife feels it's important to be at a special event, ask God for the strength to be there emotionally as well as physically. That does not mean that if her side of the family is engaging in illegal or immoral things that you have to participate in any way. You can learn about what interests them or about the line of work her family members are in. The point is that you highly value your wife, and if it's an important family time for her family, then show up and show her you love her enough to be committed, even in the tough situations.

6

Faith-Building Blessing

In the book Song of Solomon, King Solomon's bride pictures their house: "The beams of our houses are cedars; our rafters, cypresses" (Song of Solomon 1:17). But guess who holds it up. Remember that God's tabernacle (his special dwelling place) had beams of cedar holding it up and rafters of cypress wood keeping out the rain. In such a house, Solomon's bride would feel secure and loved and blessed. Now if that picture doesn't hit home, let me share with you flat out that your taking your spiritual life seriously blesses your wife in incredible ways.

So here are some suggestions of how to add to your home spiritual strength, those strong cedar beams and cypress rafters that keep out the elements that can spoil or ruin your home:

➲ You be the one who says, "Hey, let's plan

better this week so that we make it to church on time."

⮕ You be the one who asks, "So what's one thing I can do to help you in getting the kids ready for church, besides sitting in the car and beeping?"

⮕ You be the one who says, "OK, at our house, we're saying grace before each meal." And then take the lead by either praying for the food before you eat or asking someone else in the family to pray at the table. But make sure you don't just delegate; you be the one praying as well, even if it's a little uncomfortable at first. Just pray conversationally, like you were thanking your friend (in this case, someone who really is your best, most faithful friend, Jesus) for providing the food and family you get to enjoy.

⮕ You be the one who says, "Honey, once a year, let's go to some kind of conference that is going to help strengthen our marriage." And then start saving for that seminar and take the lead in signing up for it.

➲ You as the father be the one who is in the bedroom and prays with the children before they go to bed. It's fine to have your wife pray as well or for you to take turns. But you pray for them too. They need to hear your voice blessing their life. That sound of you praying for your children will absolutely bless your wife's heart as well as your children's.

➲ You be the one who doesn't just flop into bed and try and set the world speed record for falling asleep. You be the one who takes your spouse's hand and prays with her. That alone (even if it's just one-sentence prayers before you hit the sack and even if you're calling in from a business trip) can do amazingly positive things for your marriage. In clinical studies, couples who pray together really do stay together at dramatic rates!

Hated-Chore Blessing

Housework is something that makes up a big part of family life. Because of this reality, there are tons of ways you can bless your wife by stepping up and pitching in with chores. Here are some ideas for you:

➲ Be committed to do a chore for her that she hates to do, even if it's something you hate more! Learn to vacuum. Learn how the dishwasher works, and do the dishes at least some of the time. Help your kids do their homework, even math. Learn how the washing machine works and occasionally do the laundry. And if you don't know how a machine works, ask to be shown how to use it.

➲ Every few months, declare a Mom's National Holiday, a whole day when your wife does not have to do a single chore. She can sleep in. Not make the bed. Take a long shower and use up all the hot water. Not cook or do the dishes. In short, it's just a day to say that you and the kids express high value for all your wife does for the family. The holiday is a day for your wife to rest and be celebrated and for the rest of the family to get to do all that your wife does. Just watch the appreciation grow for her when you do that. Especially if the kids have to eat your cooking!

8

Care-for Her-Interests Blessing

 Be committed to your wife's education, her Bible study meetings, and/or her dreams, not just your own. It's not easy for both a husband and wife to develop careers or interests or educational goals, or to dig deeper into God's

Word, or to pursue their dreams or hobbies that they've set aside for the kids or their spouse. But it's important to actively show that you care about your wife's interests:

- ⭮ If your wife starts back to school, arrange your schedule and budget so that she gets started, even if the start is just one class at a community college or the free course she's always wanted to take at a community center.

- ⭮ If your wife would love to be in a Bible study that meets at night, make the sacrifice to watch the kids and get her the materials she needs.

- ⭮ Ask her what dream or hobby she put aside when "life happened" that you could help her pick back up.

9

Attitude-Check Blessing

 Make it a priority to be committed to dealing with those habits and attitudes in your life that you know God isn't thrilled about. This comes with a pretty positive benefit! If you'll clean up those impurities and things in your life that you know God doesn't like, you may just see your wife become more attracted to you physically! Here's why I say that: it's based on God's word!

In the Song of Solomon, Solomon's wife says, "May he kiss me with the kisses of his mouth!" (Song of Solomon1:2). I can remember speaking at a Promise Keeper's conference years ago in Tampa, Florida. There were over 50,000 men packed into what used to be called the Thunderdome (now called Tropicana Field), a huge stadium, and I was speaking on being a husband who blessed his wife. So I read that verse and asked those 50,000 men, "Men, how many of you would like to go home and hear your wife say, 'Get over here and don't just kiss me once, but smother me with kisses!'? If you'd like to hear that when you get home, then let me hear an 'Amen!'" And believe me, that place became the *Thunder*dome!

But then I quieted them down and said, "But hang on. Let's look at God's Word and see why she wants to kiss him so much. Solomon's wife goes on to say, 'May he kiss me with the kisses of his mouth. For your oils had a pleasing fragrance. Your name is like purified oil'" (Song of Solomon 1:3).

Here's what she means by that word picture of purified oil and wanting to get physical. She wants to kiss him—repeatedly—because of his character, not his bank account or biceps or who his father was or what he could give her. Even as the king, he could give her a lot of things! What makes her want to be physically responsive to him is his name (which in Hebrew stood for who he was) and the fact that it was like purified oil. I saw what this meant years ago, during my first trip to the Holy Land.

Near Nazareth, which is where Jesus grew up, our tour guide pointed out how they used to purify oil back in Jesus' day. First, someone would build scaffolding over a natural well or indentation in a rock or large stone that could collect liquid. Then people would smash up the olives and pour the unrefined olive oil on a top tray of rocks held by the scaffolding. The oil would seep through that top tray, and as it dripped down, many of the biggest impurities would be taken out. Then the oil would drip onto a second tray, this one filled with smaller rocks, and finally a third tray with a layer of sand. By the time it seeped through and collected at the bottom, it was purified. The process had gotten rid of enough of the impurities so that it could be used to light a lamp. Do you get the picture of what "your name is like purified oil" means now? If not, let me help you.

In my counseling practice, I could name a hundred times when a couple came in and at least part of their problem was their sexual relationship. And in many cases, what was causing the problem in regards to intimacy wasn't a physical problem; it was a character problem. One of them wasn't even trying to do something about an attitude or action that God's isn't thrilled about anyone doing.

For example, one man had a home-based

business, and it was clear to his wife that he was cheating his customers and lying to creditors. His wife was right there—in the home—listening to him lie and take advantage of people. What a shock that when they came into my office, she had lost all her romantic feeling for him.

Coming from a broken home and filled with anger as a kid before I came to Christ, I still struggled with my tone of voice early in our marriage. Then I really set out to work on both my sarcasm and my tone of voice. Amazingly, as I worked on those character issues—which adversely affected Cindy—she moved much closer to me!

Husband, you bless your wife when you focus on getting the impurities out of your life. You'll never be perfect. I'm certainly not. But know this: in a marriage, a woman has a terrible time freely giving herself to someone she doesn't trust or respect. So here are a few suggestions to curb a wrong attitude:

⮑ Be willing to say, "My tone of voice was really bad. I'm sorry. I'm going to work on that." And then do work on it, with the help and strength of the Lord and your wife.

➲ Follow through on a chore, instead of saying, "Yes, I'll do it" and getting busy with your own things and not getting it done. If you tell her you're going to do something, do it.

➲ Ask your bride, "What is one thing I could do, you think, to be a better husband, father, or follower of Jesus? Just one." And she can tell you. And then that one area is a great point to start working on. It's a way of saying, "I'm committed to bless you."

Secret-Message Blessing

I grew up not knowing Jesus. In my single-parent home, my brothers and I did not see modeled ways a husband could bless his wife with his touch. But years later, I met a family—my Young Life leader's family—who really lived out their faith. And it was obvious that this husband and wife loved each other. Here are two ways they said "I love you" by using loving touch:

- ➲ Before eating a meal at this Young Life leader's home, everyone at the table would hold hands and pray. For the first meal I had at the home of this former college football player, his family and several of us guys from the football team sat around the table, and I happened to sit next to my Young Life leader, Doug Barram. That was the first time I had ever held hands with a grown man. And it was a powerful picture of how a family, holding hands, can communicate through touch that "We're connected!" even as they prayed.

- ➲ Doug and his wife also had a secret way of saying "I love you." If they held hands when they were walking or in a movie theater or at church, one of them would squeeze the other's hand gently three times. Once for *I*, once for *love*, and once for *you*. And the other person would then squeeze (gently) the other person's hand four times: *I, love, you, too.*

I grew up in Arizona, where it's OK to hug your horse, not your wife. But this simple, three-four squeeze of the hands is a great way to say—without words—a blessing through loving touch. Set up a secret way to say "I love you" with your wife, and don't hesitate to hold hands when you pray.

Sit-a-Little-Closer Blessing

Get moving towards your spouse by sitting next to her, not just across from her. At least once a week, look for a time when you can sit next to your wife at a table or on the couch—and just be near her.

- Sometimes sit on the same side of the booth in a restaurant.

- If she's sitting on the couch and watching television, sit next to her, no matter what channel is on.

➲ Give her a five-minute back rub with no strings attached!

12

Shoulder-to-Cry-On Blessing

My mother was in tremendous pain from rheumatoid arthritis for much of my childhood, but she had an incredible attitude and simply didn't cry or complain. So I wasn't used to tears. My wife, Cindy, however, can be moved to tears while watching a movie, talking to someone on the phone, or listening to one of the kids share a trial they've gone through. God has just given her a soft heart. If that's true with your wife, then don't do what I did when we were first married. The show of emotion was my signal to step away. I thought I was giving her emotional distance and some space to get things back under control. What I didn't know was that when I'd go into the garage or drive off to get a coffee or a soft drink, she was left feeling alone and rejected, and she felt like I didn't care.

If your wife cries, then as uncomfortable as it might be for you, see if she will let you take her hand or put your arm around her. I thank God that Cindy asked me one day, as she started to tear up and I started to pack up and head to the garage, why I felt I had to leave when she was sad. But it was how she said it that finally broke through and helped me see that I was being hurtful by subtracting my loving touch.

"John," she said, "What would you think about someone on a football team you played on who walked out of the huddle. He just walked away from the rest of the team before the play was called." I said I didn't think that person should be on the team. "Then why do you walk out on me when I start crying?" she said. That led to one of the most honest—if painful—conversations we've ever had. And it was the first time I really understood that she didn't need me to step away when there were tears; she needed me to step towards her and to hold her hand or put my arm around her.

Your wife is unique. But before you just assume that she doesn't need your touch when times are tough, try stepping towards her quietly. Taking her hand softly. Putting your arm around her to comfort her.

13

Gentle-Words Blessing

 Bless your wife by bringing home a powerful biblical truth: "A gentle answer turns away wrath" (Proverbs 15:1, NIV).

I remember hearing in a counseling class how many couples who get in heated arguments will, even without realizing it, put the kitchen island or a family-room table between them as their voices are raised. And that's when I realized I had been doing the same thing. So I came home and asked God—and asked Cindy—to hold me accountable to initiate the peace when during an argument, things go from the discussion stage to the dishonor stage.

Think about this for a moment more: biblically, the strong person always initiates the peace. It's absolutely true. For example, Romans 5:8 says, "God shows his love for us in that while we were still sinners, Christ died for us" (ESV).

Now link that thought with being soft and with loving touch. The next time things heat up between the two of you, remember that you bless your wife when you choose to be strong, and you do that by choosing to be soft as you initiate the peace.

For Cindy and me this meant that I would step towards her and ask, "So can we stop and cool off a bit? And then let's talk about this holding hands."

What a difference! After that cooling-off period, we'd sit or stand and hold hands. We'd have the same talk about the same issue that had sparked so much contention. But it was a totally different conversation! When we held hands, it was so hard to get back to the same very bad place we'd been!

You bless your wife when you use softness to take the heat out of a discussion, and one way to do that is by holding hands, particularly, as you talk through difficult issues.

14

Care-about-Her-Past Blessing

 Time goes by so quickly, yet a powerful way to communicate your love and blessing is by going retro—helping your wife know that you value her past, that you value knowing not only who she is but who she was as well. You bless your wife when you express high value today by showing an interest in her past. You can do that by doing several things:

⮑ Over 165 times in the Bible, you find the word remember. And most of those times, it's used to remember God's faithfulness, his covenant, his love for us. So look for those positive things you can recall with your wife, like writing out the story of your courtship for a special date or anniversary. Write it out as you remember it, and then ask her to either confirm or correct the story. Either way, it's a hit to talk about how God first drew you together.

➲ Get excited about going to her class reunion. Actually, I enjoyed Cindy's high school reunion way more than mine. What I didn't realize was it blessed her when I showed an interest in who she had been and the people who had been important to her. As you seek to serve and be a student of your spouse to bless her, start by bringing up and remembering with her things in her past that were positive.

➲ Drag out her high school yearbook some night. Ask her to talk you through who some of the important people in her life had been at the time and the things she did and liked back then.

15

Honor-Your-In-Laws Blessing

 You bless your wife when you honor her father and mother.

If you're serious about expressing high value to your wife, then look for ways to praise her parents. Of course, the first of the Ten Commandments with a promise is "Honor your father and your mother, as the LORD your God commanded you, that your days may be long, and that it may go well with you in the land that the LORD your God is giving you (Deuteronomy 5:16, ESV). That's quite a promise! But in all honesty, there are some of us who have had parents who were or are challenging to honor. Keep in mind, however, what that word *honor* means. My father, for example, was an alcoholic who walked out on our family when I was two months old. For years I hated him and didn't even know him. But then I became a Christian and realized that as long as I hated him, I was becoming just like him!

I like to think of the word *forgiveness* in terms of "untying the knot." Understanding that truth was life-changing for me. When I hated my father (and even when I became a Christian and just "intensely disliked him"), I wasn't free to choose life and movement towards God's best! I was all "tied up in knots!" In part, that's why Jesus was so insistent that we must choose to forgive "seventy times seven" times (Matthew 18:22)! We're the ones who are set free when, by God's love and strength, we choose to forgive someone, even someone who perhaps didn't come close to blessing us when we were young.

Again, I'm not advising you to excuse bad, wrong, or terrible behavior. Even after I forgave my father, I would never let him drive our kids in the car if he had been drinking. But you simply cannot hate your way to freedom. So since that's true, here are some suggestions for honoring your in-laws:

⤷ If your wife's parents were (or are) wonderful, loving, godly people, then sit down with your spouse and write them a letter that blesses and thanks them for what they did to encourage and raise your wife to be who she is today!

➜ If a parent wasn't so great, then still look for something positive that was a part of that person's life story. For example, my father served in the 41st Division in the Pacific during World War II. His unit was called the Bushwhackers, because they fought their way through so much jungle and through so many islands. He was wounded three times and received the Bronze Star for carrying a wounded soldier through intense enemy fire to safety. That's great heroism and patriotism. So I made a shadow box containing all his military decorations. Although this shadow box now hangs on my office wall, for years it hung over the piano where our girls could see it when they practiced and took lessons. It was a "picture" of something about their grandfather that they could value and appreciate, just as I could, after I "untied the knot" and forgave him. So even if one or both of your wife's parents weren't Christian Parent of the Decade material, look for ways to honor and celebrate your in-laws.

Make sure you set aside a block of time to talk about what the two of you are going to do when her parents get old enough to need help (and the same for your parents). It may be years in coming, but it is an incredible blessing when our spouse takes a genuine interest in our parents, in loving and valuing them and planning in advance to be there for them as they grow older.

— **16** —

Birthday Blessing

 Express the high value of your wife by making a big deal about her birthday.

I know that on television and in the movies you hear women saying all the time that they don't want to be reminded of how old they are. That may be true, but the flip side of that is that odds are about one in a hundred that your wife will feel genuinely blessed if you treat her birthday as almost a national holiday. In all seriousness, I have found time and again that when couples act ambivalently towards their spouse's birthday, there are often issues involved of stepping away that often prove to be serious to the relationship. That may sound strong, but don't kid yourself into thinking that skipping your wife's birthday is a minor thing. It's like calling her by the wrong name in public or showing such selfishness that because it's not *your* birthday, hers isn't such a big deal. It *is* a big deal. Fun suggestions:

- ➲ Find something that was printed on her birthday—literally her birth date—like a *Life* magazine dated with whatever your spouse's birthday happens to be.

- ➲ Look for ways on special birthdays to surprise her with letters from family and friends sent to you at work, so you can put them into a scrapbook for her.

Picture Perfect Blessing

 Have a picture of your wife on your desk at work and at home (or on the wall, so you can see it as you look up from your desk). It seems like such a small thing. But it isn't. What people put around them is a reflection of what's important to them. This is why, in expressing your wife's high value, you should think seriously about also doing the following:

➲ Carry a picture of your wife and your children in your wallet.

➲ Use a mug with a family picture on it.

➲ Make sure you have a picture of the two of you as well as a photo of just your wife. (And keep in mind that while on vacation, don't just take pictures of scenery. Get a trusted person to take a picture of the two of you at memorable sites as well.)

Calendar Blessing

 Bless your wife by setting aside a Calendar Day—a meeting time with your bride.

I remember being at a party years ago and talking with another couple about something Cindy and I were going to be doing that was coming up. "I just love going to parties with you," Cindy said after the couple had left. "That's the only way I find out what's going on in our schedule!" If that sounds anything like you, then I suggest you do what we did: we set up something we called Calendar Sunday.

Right after dinner on Sunday night, before we got the kids to bed or turned on the tube, we would sit down together with our calendars. We'd talk first about the previous week and any "open loops" we needed to close. And then we'd look at the new week. It was incredible to me how something so close to being a business meeting was such a blessing to my wife. We've kept this up year after year, so I know for sure that getting on the same page is a great way of drawing closer and blessing your spouse.

19

Next-Generation Blessing

 Teach your children to express high value to their mother, even when they're very young.

Here are a couple of ways to bless your wife that involve your modeling and coaching your children to do as you've done, to value their mother as you've valued your wife!

➲ At Christmas, give each child a new $20 bill that can only be spent on their mother. This was a suggestion by a world-class friend named Darrell Herringer. Darrell walked up to me at church one Sunday in early December and handed me two crisp $20 bills. "This isn't for you," he said. "It's one $20 bill for Kari [our favorite oldest daughter who was seven at the time] and one for Laura [our favorite younger daughter who was three]." He went on to share how he had started this with his four daughters decades ago. So began a tradition in our home to bless my wife that is now two decades old for us! On Christmas Eve, when Cindy is wrapping presents, I head to the mall with both girls. They have one assignment on this trip: look for the most creative way or thing they can spend that $20 on for their mother, my wife. Even with the way inflation has eroded the value of $20 after two decades, these two presents from her girls are highlights for her. And it's a great way for you to bless your wife as well.

- ⮕ Make sure you step in and stop any child from verbally dishonoring, being abusive to, or using foul language with your wife. It's not cute when a child dishonors a parent, but it's amazing how many counseling situations I've been in with parents where one parent is being incredibly dishonored (verbally and even sometimes physically) and the other parent steps away and does nothing to stop the dishonor. We avoided that sort of thing by using a simple family contract:

TRENT FAMILY CONTRACT

The Trent family members agree that we will do the following:

Honor God by loving him, going to church, and reading about him.

Honor each other by making sure we use words that bless, not subtract.

Honor other adults and children who God brings into our home.

Honor our pets.

These very simple family rules were drawn up and explained, and then all four family members signed the contract. It was posted on the refrigerator (because important things always go on the refrigerator), and it became a tremendous tool for helping us raise our children to honor the Lord, their parents, their friends, and their pets. And it gave me a great tool for stepping in—because I have their signature on it—and enforcing a time-out or other penalty for the children lipping off to their mother.

➲ On Mother's Day, teach your children that Mother's Day is Zero Chore Day for Mom. From the time your children are five or six years old, start getting them used to doing something nice for Mom. It doesn't have to cost anything, so it's not like the $20 for Christmas. Rather, look for hands-on ways that they can express their love for their mother that can give you a great way to honor and bless your wife in the process.

You're-Beautiful-Breakfast Blessing

While I have mentioned that you should focus on more than just your wife's physical traits when you praise her, it is vital that you praise your wife as being beautiful physically to you as well. When you marry, your wife becomes your standard of beauty. Making sure that she knows that she captivates you will do wonders for the intimacy of your marriage, and it will bless her heart. There are so many women who grow up never hearing that they are beautiful, and they are beautiful. God made your wife the gorgeous woman that she is.

As a fun way to let her know that you think she is beautiful just the way God made her, do a you're-beautiful-without-makeup breakfast: "kidnap" your wife before she has a chance to put on her morning makeup (if she wears makeup) and make sure she knows she's beautiful to you, even without her makeup!

Fortune-Cookie Blessing

Start a tradition that begins the next time you go out to eat Chinese food. No matter what the fortune cookie that you eat at the end of your meal says, always open yours and tell her, "My fortune cookie says, 'I have an incredibly wonderful and beautiful wife.'" Every time, from here on out, for the rest of your life. And make sure you say it, no matter who the other people at the table with you are. Sure, it's a small thing, but like Proverbs 16:24 says, "Pleasant words are a honeycomb, sweet to the soul and healing to the bones". All that from a fortune cookie . . . and choosing to say it.

Communication-Card Blessing

Hand your wife a Thirty Minutes of Communication Card she can redeem anytime she needs to talk.

I was the worst at having anything resembling a long conversation with my wife when we began our marriage. I didn't want to talk; I wanted to just go to a movie. When we got to the car, I didn't want to talk about the movie, so I'd just turn on the radio to see what sports scores had come in since we'd been inside. When we got home, I was always too tired to sit down and talk, and in the morning . . . I'm not a morning person, and besides I had to go to work! I always had an excuse (a poor one) for why now isn't the right time to talk. And in part, it's because I'd never seen a couple really sit down and talk through something. Maybe it's adult ADD (attention deficit disorder) tendencies, but for me, just sitting and talking wasn't nearly as fun as doing something. But doing something is talking with your wife. Which means more than just a quick weather-report type of conversation ("How's it going?" "What's up?" "Whatever you think." "Do we have to talk about this now?").

So give your wife a Thirty Minutes of Communication Card that she can use at a time that works best for her, where the two of you are going to sit down for thirty minutes (or more) and talk about something that's important to her: the kids, your future, her parents, your retirement (even though you just got married and that's decades away)—whatever she wants to talk about. Then make sure to hand the card back to her, so she can use the card again.

23

Banner Blessing

Bless your wife by hanging over her a "banner" that says you bless her.

Do you have a friend who loves wearing their team colors and logo? I mean, really loves it? They've got their team sticker on their car (check). They've got their team key chain (check), T-shirts plural (check), leather portfolio with the school name (check), mini-football helmet (check), luggage tags (check)—you get the idea. I can check every one of those statements because of my Texas Christian University Horned Frog junk (as Cindy calls it). But it's not that. It's important stuff. And it says, "Sure when I was at TCU, we didn't win one game in two years. But today we're in the Top 10 in the country." And I've got the junk to prove it!

Would that I was that "checked out" with my bride. But I have worked hard all these years to hang a banner over Cindy. That's something that Solomon's bride says about her husband: "His banner over me is love" (Song of Solomon, 2:4). Wow. No wonder she feels so important and wants to be put on display. Her husband was someone who loved her so much, she felt like he was waving a banner over her that read, "Hey, look here! Look who God has given me to do life with!" Solomon praised her in public as well as in private.

So when you have the chance:

- ➲ Praise your wife for a personality strength you see her using to help or encourage someone. "You are so alert to others' feelings. It's amazing how you can pick up on what's going on with the kids or other people and step right in and encourage them."

- ➲ Praise her for finishing a task. "You did it! After putting off your degree to get these awesome kids raised, you've gone back and done it. I'm so proud of you!"

- ➲ Praise her in front of others (including friends and the kids). "Thanks for the compliment, but Cindy's the one you should thank. I did part of the work, but she really mapped everything out and made sure we got it done."

- ➲ Look for that one time during the day when there's an opening to say, "Wow, it's probably been like a year since I thanked you for being the one who does the laundry, but I just put on this T-shirt and it smells awesome. I mean, it won't for long, because I'm heading out for a run, but you take great care to make sure the kids and you and I have clean clothes. I know it's probably a drag to do, but thanks for being so faithful and helpful to us all."

Get ready to pick her up off the ground if your thanking and praising her for things shocks her the first few times.

24

Half-Time Blessing

Have a Half-Time Talk with your wife, instead of listening to talking heads tell you what you just saw.

When half-time comes the next time you watch a game, put the TV on record and go ask your wife three questions, maybe something like this:

➲ "So what's one thing you've got coming up this next week?"

⊃ "I guess that thing that's coming up is making you feel a little nervous?"

⊃ "What's one thing I could do to help you with that thing next week, besides pray for you about it?"

Actually, you can ask her three questions anytime. When you walk in the door, after dinner, in the car. Start with something going on in her world. Then follow up with a question that is a guess at how you think that issue/concern/meeting/appointment makes her feel. (She'll probably tell you if what you guess is not what she's feeling, but if she doesn't fill in the blank with how it does make her feel, ask her to do that.) Finally, after you've listened to something coming up and how she feels about it, ask her if there's any way, besides praying for her, you could be of help to her in facing or dealing with that situation/task/meeting/phone call.

And guess what. If you ask those three questions and listen to the answers, you've actually had a conversation with your wife! And by the time you've gone through all three, she feels heard and more valued.

25

Character Blessing

 Find ways to bless your wife by pointing out her incredible character. It means so much to a woman when you compliment more than her physical attributes and instead give attention to her character. Here's a suggestion for you:

➲ Write down and then read to your wife some specific things you love and appreciate about her that match the letters of her name! Do that by writing down a word for each letter of her name and then an example of when she demonstrated that trait. Remember, these are character traits, not physical traits.

Here's an example of what I mean:

C = **Courageous** (You flew home by yourself from Norway.)

I = **Industrious** (You are *so* good at staying on top of things.)

N = **Needed** (I need you so much and am thankful God gave you to me.)

D = **Dependable** (If you say you'll do something, I never worry it won't get done.)

Y = **Young at heart** (You're still ready to jump in and do fun things.)

Yes, it's corny and somewhat lame. But watch how much it means to her when you're out at a no-big-deal dinner and you tell her before the food comes that you've written something about her. Then read it to her. Then watch her take in those words—that praise—and she'll feel like Solomon's bride who wanted to be put on display.

26

Questions Blessing

Ask your wife some great questions that the two of you can talk about.

Some studies have shown that women speak, on average, over twice as many words during the day than men! This means that a man may have already used up all his words when he gets home, and the woman is just getting started! Your willingness to engage her in using some of those words each day can go a long way towards building the blessing into her life.

Here are some great questions to ask her that almost always can be the start of a good conversation:

- ➲ "What is the most important issue facing our child today?" Then talk about how you can help with that issue.

- ➲ "So what's an area in your life you'd like to grow in?" Then as a follow-up, ask, "So what's one area in my life you think I could work on or grow in?"

➲ "What is one thing I could do to make our marriage better or stronger?"

➲ "What's a book you're reading that you can tell me about?"

➲ "Walk me through a television show you recently watched, something you know that I'm probably never going to watch. Tell me why you like it so much." You might find that you've been missing something you really might enjoy.

Future-Plans Blessing

To give your wife something to look forward to with you, set up times in the future when just the two of you will spend time together.

One way to do this is to hand your wife an Upcoming Adventure with My Wife card, a three-by-five-inch index card on which you've written four things the two of you could do together. Also provide a space for her to write in her own idea, if she doesn't choose one of the four you've provided.

UPCOMING ADVENTURE WITH MY WIFE

Four things I could do with my awesome wife:

❑ Go to [an oldies concert] that's coming to town.

❑ Take a day trip to [nearby town] to look at antiques.

❑ Take a cooking class together.

❑ Go to the state fair.

❑ An even-better idea of something to do together: _____.

After she makes her choice (or suggests something else) and you've agreed, then sit down and start planning. Maybe you'll have to save up some money or line up tickets well ahead of time. The goal here is for just the two of you to spend time together. So be careful not to form a group to go to the concert, unless she wants to do that.

Advance-Holiday-Planning Blessing

Look for potential in the holidays—thirty days ahead of time.

It's amazing how we know all year that a specific holiday is coming, but it can just sneak up on us anyway! And with that, we can get super stressed and often miss out on doing something significant we could or should have done—if we had just planned ahead!

Do this by putting in your calendar in your smartphone or computer a thirty-day reminder update of a meeting you set up with your wife. Then thirty days ahead of time, you'll get a meeting notice that pops up on your phone or computer (for example, for Thanksgiving, you'd get a notice in late October). As soon as you can after that, ask your wife to sit down and spend thirty minutes (minimum) talking about and planning activities, events, and priorities for the upcoming holiday. You can also talk about the things you *don't* want to happen, and how to avoid those.

It's amazing how much more you'll look forward to a holiday when you feel like you're planning it, instead of it driving you!

Dance-Lesson Blessing

Arrange to take dance lessons with your wife. This isn't a *Dancing with the Stars* audition. Rather, picture your son or daughter's wedding. In all likelihood, if you have children, one day they will grow up and get married. And if that's the case, if they have even a semi-traditional wedding, you will likely have to dance. It's very possible that that will be the first time since high school or junior high that you've been on the dance floor.

So plan a time when you and your wife will take dance lessons together. And before or after your lesson, talk about each child, about your plans and dreams and prayers for each child. And pray for God's preparation for the very person God has for your child to grow up and marry. I know it seems so far away if you have young kids. But that day comes in a blink. You can't start too early. And if there's not a marriage happening anytime soon, then set up a time when the two of you can use those really cool dance moves as a couple, like at a special dinner or event.

Lots-of-Little-Things Blessing

We've talked a lot already about the way small things can have lasting, often life-long, impact. So here are more kick-starters for you to think about doing to bless your wife:

➲ Get an audio book you both want to listen to and listen to it on a car trip or listen to it together for twenty minutes each night.

➲ Do a family fire drill. And make sure your wife has and knows how to use a fire extinguisher. Home fires happen, and not just to other people.

➲ Share the responsibility for the kids to wear safety equipment. Don't just make her be the only one who says, "Put on your helmet." And make sure you put on a helmet yourself, even if you wore a helmet in the service and don't feel you need a bike helmet now. You do, if you love and value and want to bless your family.

➩ Make sure your will and trust are up to date. It's amazing to me how much security a simple will or a trust can provide for a wife, especially when there are children and assets involved. Having been a family pastor in three different churches over the years, I've done my share of marrying and burying. And it has absolutely shocked me how many times the person who dies without a will isn't the eighty-year-old; it's the thirty-five-year-old who died while doing extreme mountain biking or the forty-three-year-old whose private plane's engine just froze and the resulting crash took his life. You bless your wife when you plan for her future (and that of your kids) by, if possible, having an insurance policy and certainly by having a will and legal paperwork that reflects the decisions you two make for your children, property, and health!

- Make sure the doors and windows in your house or apartment have adequate locks. That's a great way to say, "I value you and want to keep you safe."

- Make sure your wife has an emergency car kit in her car.

- If there's only time for one of you to get in a run, tell her you'll watch the kids and let her go. (And get up earlier the next time, because you need to stay in shape too).

- Practice good hygiene. Brush your teeth at least twice a day. Take a shower before you make love with her. Use breath mints. Comb or brush your hair. And don't make her tell you it's time to change any of your clothes, especially your socks or underwear.

- Make sure she knows the key details of a business trip, including each hotel and the number there. (Yes, you have a cell phone, but I can't tell you how often someone shuts off their cell phone at night, and an emergency call can't get through.)

- Call home every night when you're on the road and pray with her and for her at the end of your conversation.

- Make sure she has a nice dress that is two years old or less (yes, that might mean you have to save for such a dress), and take her somewhere where she can wear it.

- Once a month, do a Cave Man Night when no technology is allowed. Read together, talk together, play cards together, play a board game. But no technology. It's amazing how just one night without your cell phone or computer can strengthen and bless your marriage.

- Hand her a recipe that sounds good to you and then go with her to shop for the meal, help her cook it, and serve it to the entire family.

- Use good manners. That means no cussing or foul language. You're wrong if you think using filthy language in front of the kids and your wife is your right. It ruins their respect for you and pulls down your home, instead of building it up. If foul language has been a problem for you, set out a jar and put $1 in the jar for each cuss word you utter. Be ruthless in this, and really work on your language at home and at work so that it doesn't just creep into your home and into your children.

- ⊃ Use candles one night for dinner.

- ⊃ Call ahead to the restaurant you've agreed to go to for her birthday or your anniversary and arrange for them to hand her a special dessert or something else special, like flowers or a card.

- ⊃ Get the two of you moving: exercise with your wife. Find something you like to do together, and tell yourself, *We've got to move it, move it!*

- ⊃ Before a trip—and without your spouse knowing what you've done—create a playlist of songs where the words express things you appreciate about her and about the two of you. Make sure she isn't driving when she listens to it, because it might cause her to choke up.

- ➲ Take a community college course together at a local school, just for fun.

- ➲ Take the lead in your family by doing at least one service project as a couple or family each year. Make this a must-do. It's incredible what one missions trip can do for the attitude of all the family members, especially your kids' attitude. They might "hate" their "small" room, but when they help build an entire house for a family in another country and the entire house is barely bigger than their room plus a bathroom, their attitude (and yours) will improve.

- ➲ Take a vacation day on a day that matches a day she has off, so you can spend time with her.

- ➲ Go old school and actually send her a postcard or mail her a Valentine's card, instead of emailing it.

- Support a decision she made with the kids when you weren't there (or even if you were there).

- Clean the refrigerator for her once a year.

- Give her a present that's a luxury—not simply useful.

- If your wife is a sports fan, then buy her a stadium chair with her favorite team's colors or mascot on it, and then carry it for her to and from the stadium.

- Bring home a specialty cooking utensil (like a crepe maker or specialty cheese grater).

- Throw her towel in the dryer when she's getting ready to step into the shower; then hand the hot towel to her when she steps out.

- Go for a walk together.

- Open the car door for her, even when her arm isn't broken.

- Call her during the day just to tell her you love her.

- If you're supposed to pick up the kids, be on time.

- Let her pick the colors to decorate your home.

- Send away for the latest T-shirt from her high school or college.

- Volunteer to change any overhead light for her.

- Make both sides of the bed.

- Value any pet she loves, even the cat.

- Hang up your clothes.

- If you live in snow country, after a big storm, carve out a huge heart with her initials in it in the front yard so that both she and anyone who drives by can't miss seeing it.

WHY CHOOSE TO BLESS

THE CHOICES YOU make to bless your wife, even in small ways, can be life-giving and life-changing for both of you. This is particularly true if one or both of you didn't receive or see the blessing while growing up.

Life over Death, Blessing over Curse

In Deuteronomy, the Lord says to his people, "I call heaven and earth to witness against you today, that I have set before you life and death, blessing and curse. Therefore choose life, that you and your offspring may live" (Deuteronomy 30:19, ESV).

That's one choice with two parts: (1) life over death, and (2) blessing over curse. In Scripture the word *life* means movement; things that are alive are moving towards someone or something. The word *death* means to step away. That's a word picture of your first choice as a husband.

Are you going to step towards your wife—with appropriate touch, with spoken words that attach high value, by picturing a special future for her and showing her your genuine commitment? Or are you going to choose to step away—because of work, because you just don't know how to bless her, or because you never saw your father bless your mother?

Know this: what keeps us choosing to step towards our spouse is having made that first foundational choice for life in Christ! When we choose life in him, Jesus tells us, "I came that [you] may have life and have it abundantly" (John 10:10, ESV). That's LIFE in all capitals!

So when you choose Jesus as your Lord and Savior—that foundational, empowering, life-changing choice—you start moving towards his best! The new life Jesus gives you when you choose him gets you moving towards godly things—towards being more like Jesus each day—towards others in service, love, and commitment! The abundant life he offers you gives you his power and strength to keep moving towards your spouse in a positive way—even on those days (or seasons) when it's tough or difficult to do so or when you really feel like stepping away. Even if you yourself never got the blessing or saw the blessing being given growing up, you can change the pictures of your life story! Jesus gets you unstuck and moving towards him—and towards others!

So are you going to step towards or step away from the Lord? To step toward or away from your spouse? If you choose to step away from your spouse, instead of moving towards her, on an earthly level, you'll see your marriage start dying by degrees.

I see this every day in my counseling practice. My day job is being the Gary D. Chapman, Chair of Marriage and Family Ministry and Therapy at Moody Theological Seminary. That's a very long title, but what it means is that I get to counsel couples and train counselors who can help couples make that choice for life in Jesus and get moving towards each other.

I feel I have the best job on the planet, but the most challenging things I see each day are those awesome couples who started out stepping towards the Lord and towards each other, but then something happened. One spouse felt offended by something the other said or did, and slowly, but then more quickly, one spouse decided to start emotionally—and soon physically—stepping away from the other. And if that couple continues heading down that path, they'll wake up one day to find that they've quit looking for light and love from the source of life and are "suddenly" miles away from each other emotionally. They'll find that they're like the church of Ephesus described in Revelation: "[They] abandoned the love [they] had at first" (Revelation 2:4, ESV).

A Way Back

So what if your marriage has deteriorated to the point where you wonder if there's anything left? There is a way back to happiness and wholeness in a marriage. There's a biblical path your family can walk that leads you towards fulfillment, love, and peace. It's the way of blessing—small actions like the thirty examples you've read that you can draw on to communicate genuine love and acceptance to your wife; small actions that add up to big results.

Two Word Pictures

In Scripture, *to bless* suggests two pictures. The first is that of bowing the knee. This doesn't mean you have to bow literally to your spouse! That would be a little strange and confusing! But it's a picture of your acknowledging—which bowing did in olden times and still does in some cultures—that you are in the presence of someone who's extremely valuable. In this case, it's your spouse who you've chosen to bless.

With the hundreds of couples I've sat with over the last forty years, I have yet to meet with one who didn't start off thinking the other person had great worth and value. Yes, love can be blind, but the feeling they had was "this person is nothing short of great." And that's a great starting point!

When the church at Ephesus headed off in the wrong direction and drifted away from their first love for Jesus, he called them back: "Remember therefore from where you have fallen" (Revelation 2:5, ESV). He didn't say, "OK, spend all your time thinking about the lowest point in your relationship with me." His advice on how to rebuild and regain what they'd lost wasn't to focus on their failures or their disappointments. Instead, Jesus called them back to when they valued him highly: "Remember from where you've fallen." In other words, "Remember when you were looking up!"

You don't fall from the lowest point in your life! Jesus tells us to look up and remember when things were at their best—when we were on the right road! When we were choosing to bless our spouse, almost without trying, because we felt so strongly that this person was someone of great worth and value! And if you feel like that's *not* where you are today, keep this in mind: actions dictate feelings—not the reverse.

In other words, when you choose to act like someone has great worth or value—like you did when you first married—you will find your *feelings* for them will begin to follow. But never the reverse. If you just sit and wait until you feel like blessing or valuing your wife, get ready for a long wait!

Husband, I'm asking you to act in a way that demonstrates that the person God has placed in the middle of your life story is someone with great value. Jesus talked about this when he said, "Where your treasure is, there your heart will be also" (Matthew 6:21, ESV). In short, when you start valuing something or someone, your feelings for that thing or person will begin to change as well!

The second picture of *blessing* carries the idea of weight or value—like adding coins to an ancient scale. The greater the weight, the higher the value. If our attitude is that our spouse has high value, then our actions towards them are reflected in the second picture: adding "weighty" words and actions to show value.

Think about how we bless the Lord. When we say that (or sing those words), we're really saying, "Lord, you're so valuable, I bow the knee before you." But then we add our praise to him. In short, when we bless someone, we acknowledge in our heart that that person has great worth and value, and then we act on that by adding to their life through blessings!

Because our spouse is so valuable, our blessing of them adds to their life, like adding a coin to a scale. It means we make the decision to add more value to them: "Since God has given you to me as my wife, my completer, helper, lover, companion, and friend, I'm choosing to add to your life."

And as C. S. Lewis said, when you choose to do some of these small, positive things, you'll see good "increase at compound interest" and you'll bless your marriage, your family, and your future!

Blessing is a hugely better choice than its opposite: to curse. (Remember, we're to choose blessing over curse.). In Scripture, the word *curse* suggests doom or at the very least misery; it's as if life-giving water is taken away from someone. That's a terrible picture. I'm not going to spend time focusing on how we subtract from others. That just comes naturally from our fallen nature and our poor choices. We can choose to subtract our love and encouragement. And let me emphasize that it is a choice, not something anyone made us do.

My prayer for you is that you will choose life over death, blessing over curse. And I pray that you'll live out that choice starting today!

Starting a Revolution

Reading this book and putting its ideas to use (and perhaps getting another copy and sharing it with a friend or relative who will hold you accountable to be a man of blessing for your wife) can be nothing short of *revolutionary*. That means that blessing your wife can bring about a fundamental or major change in the relationship you have with your wife and the culture you establish in your home.

It's *revolutionary* to come to Christ and to see him turn us into a new creature (2 Corinthians 5:17). It's *revolutionary* that Jesus gave up his life so that we could have eternal life (John 3:16). That same kind of revolutionary, crazy, transformational love that Jesus pours out on you who know him is nothing short of the kind of love that you're to have for your spouse! Jesus "has blessed you in the heavenly realms with every spiritual blessing in Christ" (Ephesians 1:3, NIV), and you can enjoy all of those blessings now. And you're called on to love your wife—to build into her life—to choose to bless her as well!

LET THE
BLESSING BEGIN

HUSBAND, YOU HAVE a sphere of influence with your wife that no one else has. I pray that you are encouraged to use that influence to bless your wife like no one else can. Through meaningful touch, spoken words of high value, picturing a special future, and an active commitment to your wife, you can pass on the incredible gift of the blessing. I hope that you have found some helpful ideas in this book as you embark on a journey to bless your wife and to bless others. I'm praying for you on your journey.

Lord, may you bless this man who holds this book. Thank you that he's read it and that he's committed now to start in to bless his wife. Lord she is a gift from you.

No matter the challenges or trials this couple has been through or may encounter, Lord, may this man know the truth of how actions dictate feelings, not the other way around. His decision and choice to bless his wife is something you will honor.

Finally, Lord, help this husband to know that small things can begin to change everything. You, Jesus, talked about that when you shared that faith the size of a tiny mustard seed can move a mountain [Matthew 17:20]. Lord, may these small things (and other similar things this husband comes up with) bring great things to his marriage as he gives and lives the blessing.

> *Now, Lord, may these small ideas and thoughts be like that God-blessed mustard seed that, based on your love and blessing, blooms into a new season of love and life for this couple. And may every new season of life for this couple be one filled with your light, love, life, and blessing.*

Notes

1. This section adapted from John Trent and Gary Smalley, *The Blessing*, (Nashville: Thomas Nelson, 2011)

Bring the Blessing to Your Home

A spouse's or a parent's approval affects the way people view themselves. You can give your spouse and/or your children the gift of unconditional acceptance the Bible calls the blessing. This set of four short booklets is packed with tips on what the blessing is, and each booklet gives 30 ideas on how to give it to those around you. Even if you didn't get the blessing as a child, you can learn to give it to others.

Author John Trent is a Christian psychologist and co-author of the million-copy bestselling book, *The Blessing.* He shares his own story of his father's abandonment, and how he learned to give the blessing to his children.

Paperback, 112 pages, 4.5 x 6.5 x .25 inches

30 Ways a Father Can Bless His Children
9781628622775   4077X

30 Ways a Mother Can Bless Her Children
9781628622805   4078X

30 Ways a Husband Can Bless His Wife
9781628622836   4079X

30 Ways a Wife Can Bless Her Husband
9781628622867   4080X

Get 10 more tips!
FREE! Download 10 More Ways to be a Blessing to Those Around You.
Go to — BlessingChallenge.com